THIS BULLET GF

A Little Additional
inspiration

- BUDGETS/FINANCIALS
- GROCERY LISTS
- MEAL PLANNING
- FITNESS LOG
- WEEKLY CHORES
- COURSE PLANNING
- SELF CARE
- APPOINTMENTS
- HOLIDAY SHOPPING LIST
- BOOKS TO READ
- IMPORTANT DATES
- BIRTHDAYS
- SLEEP TRACKING
- WATER TRACKING
- DEADLINES
- RECIPES
- ACCOMPLISHMENTS

- DOODLING
- EXAMS
- GOALS & DREAMS
- CALENDAR
- MEDICINE
- HABIT TRACKING
- DAILY TO-DO LISTS
- DIARY WRITING
- MEMORIES
- STORYWRITING
- TRAVEL NOTES
- TRAVEL PLANS
- SONG LISTS
- SCRAPBOOING
- PARTY PLANNING
- BUCKET LIST
- AND MUCH MORE

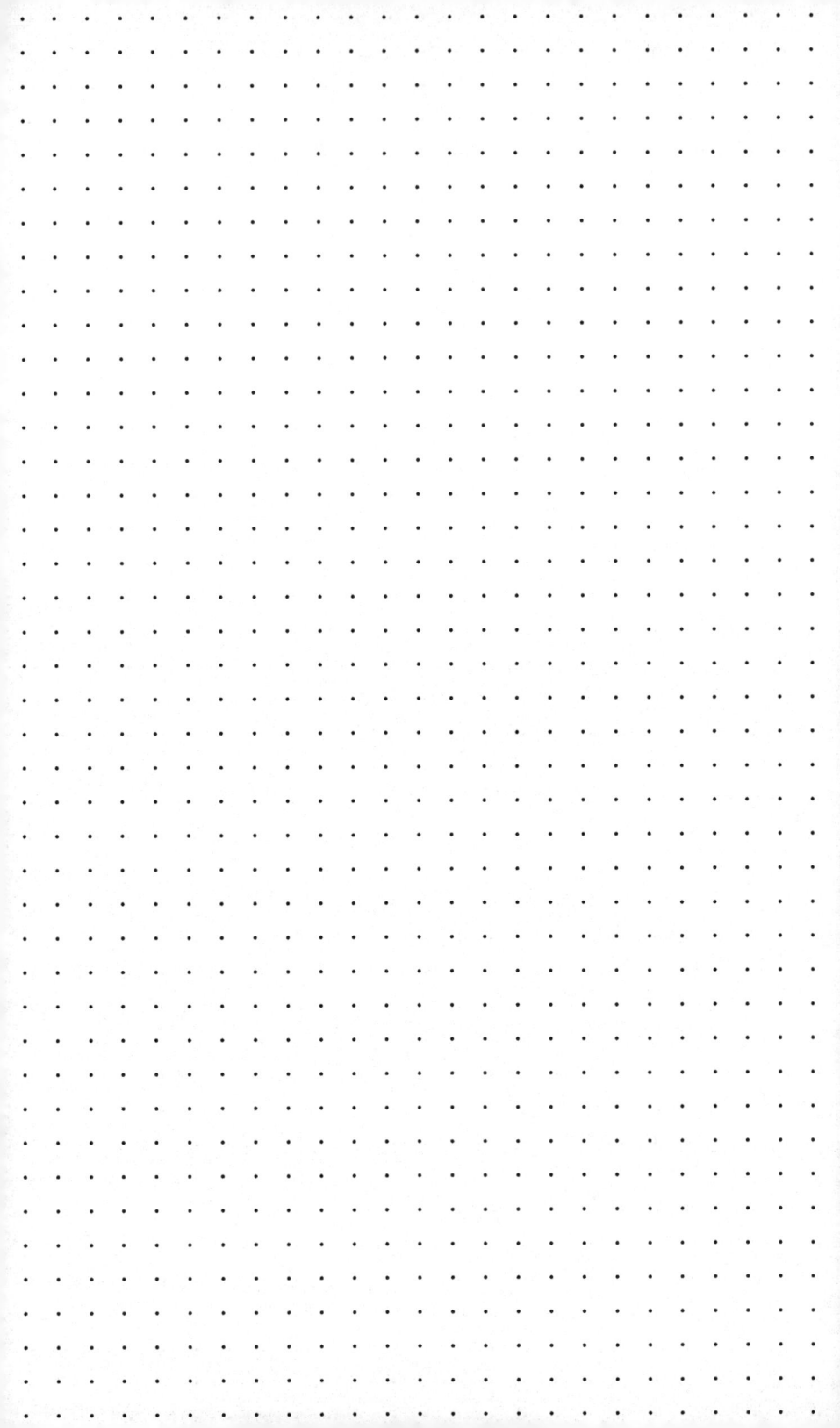

Made in the USA
Las Vegas, NV
10 September 2021